Ruth & Esther

Courageous Faith

A Bible Study Guide Journal for Women & Men

By:

Christopher S. Coopersmith

Part of the *Guiding Scripture* series

GET A FREE EBOOK: THE THREE LETTERS OF JOHN & JUDE, DAILY PROVERBS CHECKLIST, 5 QUESTIONS TO FULLY UNDERSTAND A BIBLE VERSE, A LEADER'S DAILY CHECKLIST, AND EXCLUSIVE CHRISTOPHER COOPERSMITH MATERIAL!

Get these resources for free by signing up for the mailing list at https://christophercoopersmith.com/guiding-scripture-series/

1. A Guide to The Three Letters of John & Jude – free eBook

2. Daily Proverbs Checklist

3. 5 Questions to Fully Understand a Bible Verse

4. Leader's Daily Checklist

Plus, Exclusive Christopher Coopersmith Material!

TABLE OF CONTENTS

ABOUT THE GUIDE

S ome people are so remarkable that you must name books after them. Only two books in the Old Testament were named after women, the *Book of Ruth* and the *Book of Esther*. Both women's stories display how God ultimately has a plan for redemption. The two women lived approximately five centuries apart during different times in Israel's history, yet both played a critical role in the story of our Messiah Jesus and the Jewish nation.

Ruth and Esther were both led by God to be placed at the right place at the right time. Two extraordinary women displayed endless devotion and faithfulness to the people entrusted to them. History recorded these two heroines as people with unshakable Godly character who were pivotal in shaping the course of history.

As Christians, we are to protect the very people in our sphere of influence even though society may have deemed them expendable. We are to demonstrate our faith by acting in obedience to God's will for the greater good. We are to seek the interests of others before our own continually. We can be assured that even in the direst of circumstances where we face hardship and threats, we will be redeemed by the hands of our loving Father.

SAMPLE READING PLAN

Reading the Bible is a personal and ongoing journey. There is no "right way" to do it. It is important to pray and reflect on scripture as you go through your everyday life. Here are some suggestions to help you get started:

1. Begin with Day 1 and aim to read a chapter each day.

2. Before reading the chapter, take time to reflect on the commentary at the beginning, and pray for guidance.

3. As you read the chapter, choose the one verse that resonates with you the most.

4. Write down the verse on the following page, and journal about how you feel God is speaking to you through the chapter.

5. Repeat this process each day, allowing God's Word to speak to your heart and guide your thoughts and actions.

Remember that reading the Bible is a personal experience. Take your time, reflect, and allow the Holy Spirit to guide you on your journey.

COMMUNITY GUIDE:

God's Word is the good news to be shared with all people. As believers, we can equip ourselves with the knowledge to continually bless one another just as "iron sharpens iron." Our relationships with Christ and the church are built through prayer, support, encouragement, and ministry. This Guide is an excellent resource to connect with others and apply the teachings of God's Word to our own lives.

Together as a family, we can deepen our understanding of God's Word. Community allows us to grow together in our faith as a Christ-filled body spreading the love and grace of God to everyone we meet as lights in a darkened world. Let us embrace this opportunity to connect with one another as we serve the Lord together.

TIPS ON HOW
TO BUILD COMMUNITY:

---

ssign a Group Leader: Prior to each meeting, assign one person to lead. This can be decided by the church leadership, the organizer, or a group vote. The leader should determine how the study will be organized and outline the objectives for the day. They can also appoint a co-leader(s).

Limit Group Size: This guide is a powerful tool for building relationships, so everyone should have the opportunity to connect with others. If you have a large group of ten or more, consider breaking into smaller groups of three for more personalized prayer and discussion.

Social Media Usage: A social website is a great way to create private group pages and invite friends to participate in a Guide group.

Meet Anywhere: We should never limit ourselves to the confines of a church building. Your home and public places can quickly turn into houses of worship. In today's digital world, a "meeting" can also be a video conference.

Times to Meet: The format of the book is to meet daily and discuss each chapter. However, this routine can be flexible, such as meeting every two days, weekly, monthly, etc.

Encourage Congregation Participation: In this method, the chapter is read before the regular service. One or two people will discuss how God spoke to them. After the service, there should be an allotted time for members to discuss this in more detail. They can be assigned a group or a partner, and they can meet in a general area. This method allows everyone to have the opportunity to participate.

If you do not have a community, please send an email to gs@christophercoopersmith.com to join fellow believers in our private Facebook group.

YAHWEH, GOD, LORD

The scripture portion of this book is taken from the World English Bible Translation (WEB), which is in the Public Domain. Although God has many names and titles throughout the Bible, this translation refers to God as Yahweh. Each of God's names reveals something unique about His character. Moses may have revealed Yahweh as God's name to the Israelites. Judaism has always maintained the worship of Yahweh as the one true God, and it has not replaced Him with any other deity.

INTRODUCTION

Ruth and Esther, Two Women Crucial to God's Story

I n Old Testament times, people lived in a very male-dominated
society. Most women didn't work; instead, they stayed home and
cared for the home and their children. Men led the way in the
home, workplace, synagogue, and almost every other sphere of
influence in society. It was a very different time than what we
experience today. That's what makes the stories of Ruth and Esther so
striking: they were stories of two women who walked boldly in
strength against the tides of a patriarchal society. In doing so, they
both impacted the story of God's people in remarkable ways.

Many comparisons can be made between the two of them. Both
Esther and Ruth proved that women have the power to change the
world, too. Esther saved the Jewish people. Yes, though the people
were ultimately saved through the decree of her husband, the king of
Persia, she had to initiate the saving plan first. Without her, the Jews
would have been persecuted and annihilated by Haman. Ruth
changed the world and became part of the family line of our Savior,
Jesus.

Esther also showed us that beauty is a gift from God. Her beauty was
not the defining aspect of what she accomplished, but without her
beauty, she would not have been in the position of queen, which
ultimately allowed her to save her people. God had gifted her with

beauty, and even that trait had its role in her story. The same was true of Ruth: she got Boaz's eye with her beauty and won him over with her attractive personality. He ended up playing a crucial role in her story as well.

Esther also taught us to always have a strategy before execution and be tactful when it comes to communication. She approached the King, requesting that he and Haman attend a banquet she had prepared for them. Then Esther invited them to a second banquet before making her request. She also showed us how prayer must go before any kind of action. She prayed, fasted, and asked her people to pray for her for three days before she went to the king. God heard her prayer and used her to save the people.

Ruth's story strongly reminds us that women should depend on God and not men. Ruth had been married before, but her husband died prematurely. However, when she decided to entirely depend on God, He provided her with another husband to take care of her. Esther likewise trusted God, choosing to stand up for what was right despite the repercussions that might follow.

God blesses those who love Him and others. Ruth loved her mother-in-law and chose to be with her even though she knew she might not have anyone who would marry her, coming from an alien culture. God worked on Naomi's heart to determine the details of Ruth's and Boaz's relationship, and Naomi rewarded Ruth's kindness by planning for her future.

Ruth's story shows us how godly character should be what we are looking for when it comes to searching for a spouse. Naomi and Ruth trusted Boaz's integrity so much that they knew he wouldn't take advantage of Ruth. Boaz was touched by Ruth's virtuous character: not going after any young men but doing what was the best for the family's redemption.

There is so much to learn from the lives of Ruth and Esther! Are you ready to dive into their stories together?

THE BOOK OF RUTH

ABOUT THE BOOK OF RUTH

The book of Ruth is one of the most popular in the Bible—and rightly so. The story is one of amazing love, loyalty, and redemption. Through the story of Ruth, we see a demonstration of Jesus' redeeming love. Naomi gave us a wonderful example of how to live out the love of Christ in our everyday lives.

The story starts with a famine in Judah which causes Naomi and her family to leave their home in Bethlehem for a neighboring country Moab. By the end of the story, the famine has lifted, and Naomi returns to Judah. Little does she realize it, but she is fulfilling God's grander plan.

The book's writer is unknown, although many agree it is the prophet Samuel. Some scholars dispute this because there is mention of King David, who was born much later. Therefore, we can only surmise the book was written during the time of the Judges. Yet, no matter who wrote it, we know it is the inspired Word of God, and its message remains powerful and relevant today.

The story traces the life of a Jewish and a Gentile woman who experienced redemption from God firsthand. The same redemption is offered to everyone who chooses to turn away from their old lives and follow Jesus. The main character is Ruth, a young Moabite woman who has an undying devotion to her mother-in-law, Naomi. In the second character, Boaz, we see a godly man who treats women respectfully and demonstrates God's redemptive nature.

This Guide helps us understand the profound love demonstrated throughout the story, which brings out the reckless love of God for His children. Ruth has unbreakable love and devotion toward her mother-in-law Naomi, just as Boaz has an unshakable godly character and intense love for his wife. We also learn how to deal with strangers and the underprivileged, love bitter people, and show kindness through obedience to the law.

Read, reflect, and record daily in this journal guide how you learn to embrace the same selfless love and devotion in your everyday life.

God's Promise to Abraham

Now Yahweh said to Abram, "Leave your country, and your relatives, and your father's house, and go to the land that I will show you. I will make of you a great nation. I will bless you and make your name great. You will be a blessing. I will bless those who bless you, and I will curse him who treats you with contempt. All the families of the earth will be blessed through you" (Genesis 12: 1-4).

WHO WAS RUTH?

R uth, whose name means "friend," is remarkable in her faithfulness and devotion to her mother-in-law Naomi. Even after her husband Mahlon passes away, she remains loyal to Naomi, despite not having any children after ten years of marriage. Ruth is a Moabite and therefore is considered a Gentile or outsider. When someone in the Bible is referred to as a Gentile, what is implied is a non-covenant person, for, in the Old Testament, God only made covenants with the chosen people, the Jews. God made a covenant with Jacob to make his offspring a nation, and the twelve tribes of Israel came from him.

God said to him, "I am God Almighty. Be fruitful and multiply. A nation and a company of nations will be from you, and kings will come out of your body. The land which I gave to Abraham and Isaac, I will give it to you, and to your offspring after you I will give the land" (Genesis 35:11-12).

Ruth is a direct ancestor of Jesus Christ. This fact is interesting when we consider that she comes from a people that were despised by the Jews and not accepted in the general assembly or place of worship. "An Ammonite or a Moabite shall not enter into Yahweh's assembly; even to the tenth generation shall no one belonging to them enter into Yahweh's assembly forever" (Deuteronomy 23:3). But God always has a bigger picture in mind, and selecting a Gentile to be an ancestor of our Savior reflects His love for all people. Jesus belongs to the Gentile, just as much as to the Jew. He belongs to everyone in the world regardless of origin and nationality.

Ruth's Family Tree and Genealogy:

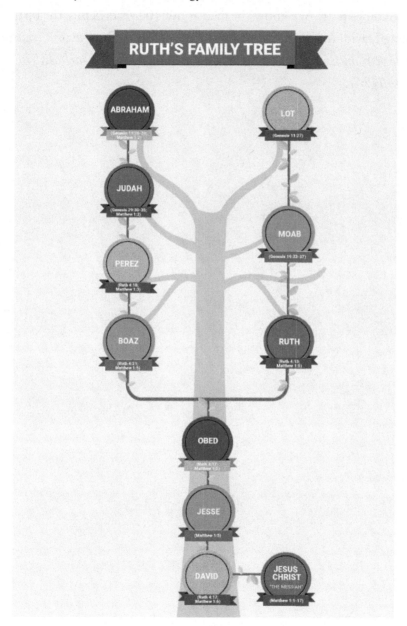

A complete scripture outline of Ruth's ancestors in the Bible is located after the conclusion of the Book of Ruth for reference.

Ruth is the great-grandmother of King David himself, from whose line comes Jesus. We know she died about 100 years before the birth of King David. *It is important to note that, although Ruth was married to a Jewish man, Mahlon, they never had children to be included in her family tree.*

CHAPTER 1
A BITTER EXPERIENCE

The story begins with Naomi, her husband Elimelech, and their two sons, Mahlon and Chilion, leaving the town of Bethlehem in Judah for Moab because of famine. Naomi's husband dies in their new land, and their sons take Moabite women as wives.

Marriage outside the Jewish faith was not prohibited under Jewish law, but marriage was forbidden with only the seven Canaanite tribes listed in Deuteronomy 7:13. However, the offspring of a marriage to a Moabite would not be allowed into the assembly for ten generations. Even in the New Testament, it is clear that God doesn't want us to be joined in marriage with those outside of the faith. "...what portion does a believer have with an unbeliever?" says Paul in 2 Corinthians 6:15. Marrying an unbeliever will change a believer's heart and walk with the Lord as the two are pulled in opposite directions because of their differing beliefs.

It is impossible to say if Naomi's sons still would have married Moabite women if their father had been alive. For ten years, their two sons would stay married until they too passed away, leaving Naomi with no grandchildren.

The Bible does not go into detail about how or why the deaths occurred. We can only speculate. It could have resulted from them moving out of the Promised Land. It was not a sin to leave the Promised Land either; only there was the possibility that one could move out of Yahweh's protection. Note that the Hebrew word for "dwell" in 1:1 suggests only a temporary stay. Therefore, Naomi and her family intended to return eventually.

Sometime after the deaths of Naomi's sons, the famine in Judah lifts, giving Naomi reason to return to her home in Bethlehem. It is important to note God is credited for lifting the famine. We are unaware of why God lifted the famine, but we know God heals lands when His people turn away from their sins. Both her daughters-in-law, Orpah and Ruth, want to go with Naomi, but she tries to persuade them that the best course of action is for them to remain in their own land. Here there would be better prospects of remarriage and family, given that they were still young. Naomi assures them that their own community and culture would be the best place for them to find husbands and start a new life. This act indicates she loved her daughters-in-law and didn't want them to suffer because of her circumstances.

After much persuasion, Orpah kisses Naomi goodbye and goes home. Naomi insists that Ruth should do the same. But Ruth clings to her. She not only insists on going with her mother-in-law but also is willing to submit to her and the God Naomi serves, rather than her pagan gods. She declares her loyalty to Naomi even to the point of death.

You can at once see the parallel between Ruth's love for Naomi and the love Jesus has for us. We reject Him and push Him away, yet He continues to knock on our doors. Jesus' name is "Emmanuel"— "God with us." Ruth's decision to stay with Naomi despite her personal wants, desires, and prospects displays the unconditional love our Savior has for us. To return that love and enjoy a fruitful life in His care, we must trust Him enough to submit to His will, placing His desires above our own. For He desires nothing but the best for us, and His ways are higher than ours.

The chapter ends with Naomi and Ruth arriving in Bethlehem. The neighbors recognize Naomi and come to welcome her. But Naomi says she is no longer the same person, and her name is now "Mara." Since "Mara" means "bitter" and "Naomi" means "pleasant," there is a sharp contrast between her former self and the personality she has taken on. We could only imagine how much pain she has had losing all of the men in her life, old or young, and apparently, she directly attributes the harsh dealings to God.

Ruth and her mother-in-law come to Bethlehem at the start of the barley harvest from April to early May, and there is plenty of work.

Ruth Chapter 1 Scripture

Naomi Becomes a Widow, and Her Sons Perish

1 In the days when the judges judged, there was a famine in the land. A certain man of Bethlehem Judah went to live in the country of Moab with his wife and his two sons.

2 The name of the man was Elimelech, and the name of his wife Naomi. The names of his two sons were Mahlon and Chilion, Ephrathites of Bethlehem Judah. They came into the country of Moab and lived there.

3 Elimelech, Naomi's husband, died; and she was left with her two sons.

4 They took for themselves wives of the women of Moab. The name of the one was Orpah, and the name of the other was Ruth. They lived there about ten years.

5 Mahlon and Chilion both died, and the woman was bereaved of her two children and of her husband.

Ruth's Loyalty and Naomi's Return to Bethlehem

6 Then she arose with her daughters-in-law, that she might return from the country of Moab; for she had heard in the country of Moab how Yahweh had visited his people in giving them bread.

7 She went out of the place where she was, and her two daughters-in-law with her. They went on the way to return to the land of Judah.

8 Naomi said to her two daughters-in-law, "Go, return each of you to her mother's house. May Yahweh deal kindly with you, as you have dealt with the dead and with me.

9 May Yahweh grant you that you may find rest, each of you in the house of her husband."

Then she kissed them, and they lifted up their voices, and wept.

10 They said to her, "No, but we will return with you to your people."

11 Naomi said, "Go back, my daughters. Why do you want to go with me? Do I still have sons in my womb, that they may be your husbands?

12 Go back, my daughters, go your way; for I am too old to have a husband. If I should say, 'I have hope,' if I should even have a husband tonight, and should also bear sons,

13 would you then wait until they were grown? Would you then refrain from having husbands? No, my daughters, for it grieves me seriously for your sakes, for Yahweh's hand has gone out against me."

14 They lifted up their voices and wept again; then Orpah kissed her mother-in-law, but Ruth stayed with her.

15 She said, "Behold, your sister-in-law has gone back to her people and to her god. Follow your sister-in-law."

16 Ruth said, "Don't urge me to leave you, and to return from following you, for where you go, I will go; and where you stay, I will stay. Your people will be my people, and your God my God.

17 Where you die, I will die, and there I will be buried. May Yahweh do so to me, and more also, if anything but death parts you and me."

18 When Naomi saw that she was determined to go with her, she stopped urging her.

Naomi's Return with Ruth

19 So they both went until they came to Bethlehem. When they had come to Bethlehem, all the city was excited about them, and they asked, "Is this Naomi?"

20 She said to them, "Don't call me Naomi. Call me Mara, for the Almighty has dealt very bitterly with me.

21 I went out full, and Yahweh has brought me home again empty. Why do you call me Naomi, since Yahweh has testified against me, and the Almighty has afflicted me?"

22 So Naomi returned, and Ruth the Moabitess, her daughter-in-law, with her, who returned out of the country of Moab. They came to Bethlehem in the beginning of barley harvest.

Chapter 1 Thoughts to Reflect Upon:

Have you ever felt abandoned by anyone or by God? Would you have stayed by Naomi's side after losing your husband if you were Ruth? Can you see how Jesus is represented in Ruth? How did you feel after reading this chapter? Did any verse stand out to you specifically?

Verse of the Day: 01/   Date:

_____

_____

_____

Journal/Notes Section-

_____

_____

_____

_____

_____

_____

_____

_____

_____

_____

_____

_____

_____

_____

_____

_____

_____

_____

CHAPTER 2
GLEANING IN THE GRAIN FIELDS

Ruth clearly has a strong work ethic, as seen from the way she works in the fields from morning to night. Here is a strong woman who exemplifies the famous Proverbs 31 woman (see below after chapter). Her character is displayed in her willingness to immediately look for menial labor in a country where she is not only a stranger but comes from a despised group, the Moabites. God blesses those who work with their hands. As Ruth is looking for the field, she "happens" to stumble into the grain fields owned by Boaz. "A man's heart plans his course, but Yahweh directs his steps," says Proverbs 16:9. God guides us into the most interesting circumstances, for He always works behind the scenes in ways we cannot fully understand.

Boaz, a relative of Naomi through Elimelech, is a key figure. Here is a man of great wealth and social standing who is immediately struck by Ruth's beauty, as well as by her selfless character. It is interesting to note that Boaz became wealthy despite the famine which caused Naomi to leave. When difficult times arise, we must seek the Lord to determine if we are to go or stay the course.

Boaz appears to be a man of wisdom, well respected by all. When he hears about Ruth's sacrifice, leaving everything she knows, he determines to give her all the help he can. He knows that as a foreigner, Ruth is vulnerable and could easily be the target of those with evil intent.

So, Ruth is blessed to have Boaz's favor and protection. He orders his men not to touch her and permits her to glean in his fields. He gives her free access to the drinking vessels and shares the midday meal with her. It is easy for people to develop a tribal mentality and only show hospitality to their own. But Boaz displays godly character by showing kindness to a total stranger, a kindness that touches Ruth's heart.

Boaz's example shines brightly today. In our world with so many highly conflicting worldviews, tribal mentalities run wild. We must walk in faithfulness to the Lord as Boaz did, extending the love of Christ to all, regardless of how different they may be from us. God loves all and wishes that His love be shown through us. That means we must serve them as Jesus would, no matter who they are or where they originated. We must keep Paul's wisdom in Galatians 3:28 close to our hearts always: "There is neither Jew nor Greek, there is neither slave nor free man, there is neither male nor female; for you are all one in Christ Jesus."

Ruth Chapter 2 Scripture

Naomi Returns to Bethlehem with Ruth

1 Naomi had a relative of her husband's, a mighty man of wealth, of the family of Elimelech, and his name was Boaz.

2 Ruth the Moabitess said to Naomi, "Let me now go to the field, and glean among the ears of grain after him in whose sight I find favor."

She said to her, "Go, my daughter."

Ruth Meets Boaz

3 She went, and came and gleaned in the field after the reapers; and she happened to come to the portion of the field belonging to Boaz, who was of the family of Elimelech.

4 Behold, Boaz came from Bethlehem, and said to the reapers, "May Yahweh be with you."

They answered him, "May Yahweh bless you."

5 Then Boaz said to his servant who was set over the reapers, "Whose young lady is this?"

6 The servant who was set over the reapers answered, "It is the Moabite lady who came back with Naomi out of the country of Moab.

7 She said, 'Please let me glean and gather after the reapers among the sheaves.' So she came, and has continued even from the morning until now, except that she rested a little in the house."

8 Then Boaz said to Ruth, "Listen, my daughter. Don't go to glean in another field, and don't go from here, but stay here close to my maidens.

9 Let your eyes be on the field that they reap, and go after them. Haven't I commanded the young men not to touch you? When you are thirsty, go to the vessels, and drink from that which the young men have drawn."

10 Then she fell on her face and bowed herself to the ground, and said to him, "Why have I found favor in your sight, that you should take knowledge of me, since I am a foreigner?"

11 Boaz answered her, "I have been told all about what you have done for your mother-in-law since the death of your husband, and how you have left your father, your mother, and the land of your birth, and have come to a people that you didn't know before.

12 May Yahweh repay your work, and a full reward be given to you from Yahweh, the God of Israel, under whose wings you have come to take refuge."

13 Then she said, "Let me find favor in your sight, my lord, because you have comforted me, and because you have spoken kindly to your servant, though I am not as one of your servants."

14 At meal time Boaz said to her, "Come here, and eat some bread, and dip your morsel in the vinegar."

She sat beside the reapers, and they passed her parched grain. She ate, was satisfied, and left some of it.

15 When she had risen up to glean, Boaz commanded his young men, saying, "Let her glean even among the sheaves, and don't reproach her.

16 Also pull out some for her from the bundles, and leave it. Let her glean, and don't rebuke her."

17 So she gleaned in the field until evening; and she beat out that which she had gleaned, and it was about an ephah of barley.

18 She took it up, and went into the city. Then her mother-in-law saw what she had gleaned; and she brought out and gave to her that which she had left after she had enough.

Ruth Tells Naomi All That Took Place

19 Her mother-in-law said to her, "Where have you gleaned today? Where have you worked? Blessed be he who noticed you." She told her mother-in-law with whom she had worked, "The man's name with whom I worked today is Boaz."

20 Naomi said to her daughter-in-law, "May he be blessed by Yahweh, who has not abandoned his kindness to the living and to the dead."

Naomi said to her, "The man is a close relative to us, one of our near kinsmen."

21 Ruth the Moabitess said, "Yes, he said to me, 'You shall stay close to my young men until they have finished all my harvest.'"

22 Naomi said to Ruth her daughter-in-law, "It is good, my daughter, that you go out with his maidens, and that they not meet you in any other field."

23 So she stayed close to the maidens of Boaz, to glean to the end of barley harvest and of wheat harvest; and she lived with her mother-in-law.

The Proverbs 31 Woman

13 She seeks wool and flax,
and works eagerly with her hands.
14 She is like the merchant ships.
She brings her bread from afar.
15 She rises also while it is yet night,
gives food to her household,
and portions for her servant girls.
16 She considers a field, and buys it.
With the fruit of her hands, she plants a vineyard.
17 She arms her waist with strength,
and makes her arms strong.
18 She perceives that her merchandise is profitable.
Her lamp doesn't go out by night.
19 She lays her hands to the distaff,
and her hands hold the spindle.
20 She opens her arms to the poor;
yes, she extends her hands to the needy.
21 She is not afraid of the snow for her household;
for all her household are clothed with scarlet.
22 She makes for herself carpets of tapestry.
Her clothing is fine linen and purple.
23 Her husband is respected in the gates,
when he sits among the elders of the land.
24 She makes linen garments and sells them,
delivers sashes to the merchant.
25 Strength and dignity are her clothing.
She laughs at the time to come.
26 She opens her mouth with wisdom.
Kind instruction is on her tongue.
27 She looks well to the ways of her household,
and doesn't eat the bread of idleness.

28 Her children rise up and call her blessed.

Her husband also praises her:

29 "Many women do noble things,

but you excel them all."

30 Charm is deceitful, and beauty is vain;

but a woman who fears Yahweh, she shall be praised.

31 Give her of the fruit of her hands!

Let her works praise her in the gates! (Proverbs 31:13-31)

Chapter 2 Thoughts to Reflect Upon:

Has God ever done something for you that you couldn't explain? Did anything ever come from you staying by someone's side to support them? Do you recognize godly character in others? How did you feel after reading this chapter? Did any verse stand out to you specifically?

Verse of the Day: 02/   Date:

_____

_____

_____

Journal/Notes Section-

_____

_____

_____

_____

_____

_____

_____

_____

_____

_____

_____

_____

_____

_____

_____

_____

_____

_____

_____

_____

CHAPTER 3
AT THE THRESHING FLOOR

I n Jewish tradition, it was the next of kin's responsibility to marry the widow and have children with her, thereby continuing his family line. In that way, his inheritance would be preserved. Boaz informs Ruth that there is a relative closer to her than him. It is possible Naomi was unaware of this fact or simply wanted Ruth to seek Boaz since she had already gained favor in his eyes. Either way, this chapter is a very compelling part of the story.

Naomi decides to play the role of cupid. Despite their age difference, Boaz's wealth and sterling character would make him the ideal match for her faithful daughter-in-law. Their ages aren't listed in the Bible. However, the Midrash indicates Boaz to be 80 and Ruth about 40. The Midrash is outside the Bible, so we are not sure of the accuracy since it is second-hand information about events in the Bible and it is not directly God's word. Most Bible scholars believe the age gap to be much smaller.

Nevertheless, there is no way for us to know for certain, and we will know more when we meet them in heaven. Ruth is very obedient to her mother-in-law. When Naomi coaches her on what to do to win additional favor with Boaz and possibly gain a husband, she follows Naomi's instructions step by step without questioning, even to the point where she would lie at the feet of Boaz in the middle of the night, risking her reputation.

Lying down with a man after working in the fields at night was a common practice for prostitutes during this season. This detail is alluded to in Hosea: "Don't rejoice, Israel, to jubilation like the nations; for you were unfaithful to your God. You love the wages of a prostitute at every grain threshing floor" (Hosea 9:1).

Our society needs more men with godly principles and self-control like Boaz. This viewpoint should be the standard by which a man treats a woman in our culture where so much darkness prevails. A beautiful woman was lying close to him, yet there was not the slightest hint of misconduct. It is past midnight, and Boaz is more concerned for Ruth's future and reputation. He doesn't take advantage of this beautiful woman who has placed herself under his wing.

The first thing he remarks to Ruth is that she did not pursue younger men and is known in the town to be a "worthy woman." Boaz sees Ruth the same way all godly men should view women who are virtuous and hard-working. He lets her spend the night with him and helps her inconspicuously leave before anyone could know she was on the threshing floor.

Just like Boaz, Jesus' earthly father Joseph was also a man of good moral character. Knowing that Mary, the woman he was betrothed to, was pregnant, he did not have intimacy with her until the birth of Jesus.

"Now the birth of Jesus Christ was like this: After his mother, Mary, was engaged to Joseph, before they came together, she was found pregnant by the Holy Spirit. Joseph, her husband, being a righteous man, and not willing to make her a public example, intended to put her away secretly. But when he thought about these things, behold, an angel of the Lord appeared to him in a dream, saying,

"Joseph, son of David, don't be afraid to take to yourself Mary as your wife, for that which is conceived in her is of the Holy Spirit. She shall give birth to a son. You shall name him Jesus, for it is he who shall save his people from their sins." Joseph didn't know her sexually until she had given birth to her firstborn son. He named him Jesus" (Matthew 1:18-21, 25).

So, we would expect the line of Jesus to be filled with honorable men. But we will see a few surprises later.

Ruth Chapter 3 Scripture

Ruth and Boaz at the Threshing Floor

1 Naomi her mother-in-law said to her, "My daughter, shall I not seek rest for you, that it may be well with you?

2 Now isn't Boaz our kinsman, with whose maidens you were? Behold, he will be winnowing barley tonight on the threshing floor.

3 Therefore wash yourself, anoint yourself, get dressed, and go down to the threshing floor; but don't make yourself known to the man until he has finished eating and drinking.

4 It shall be, when he lies down, that you shall note the place where he is lying. Then you shall go in, uncover his feet, and lay down. Then he will tell you what to do."

5 She said to her, "All that you say, I will do."

6 She went down to the threshing floor, and did everything that her mother-in-law told her.

7 When Boaz had eaten and drunk, and his heart was merry, he went to lie down at the end of the heap of grain. She came softly, uncovered his feet, and laid down.

8 At midnight, the man was startled and turned himself; and behold, a woman lay at his feet.

9 He said, "Who are you?"

She answered, "I am Ruth your servant. Therefore spread the corner of your garment over your servant; for you are a near kinsman."

10 He said, "You are blessed by Yahweh, my daughter. You have shown more kindness in the latter end than at the beginning, because you didn't follow young men, whether poor or rich.

11 Now, my daughter, don't be afraid. I will do to you all that you say; for all the city of my people knows that you are a worthy woman.

12 Now it is true that I am a near kinsman. However, there is a kinsman nearer than I.

13 Stay this night, and in the morning, if he will perform for you the part of a kinsman, good. Let him do the kinsman's duty. But if he will not do the duty of a kinsman for you, then I will do the duty of a kinsman for you, as Yahweh lives. Lie down until the morning."

14 She lay at his feet until the morning, then she rose up before one could discern another. For he said, "Let it not be known that the woman came to the threshing floor."

15 He said, "Bring the mantle that is on you, and hold it." She held it; and he measured six measures of barley, and laid it on her; then he went into the city.

16 When she came to her mother-in-law, she said, "How did it go, my daughter?"

She told her all that the man had done for her.

17 She said, "He gave me these six measures of barley; for he said, 'Don't go empty to your mother-in-law.'"

18 Then she said, "Wait, my daughter, until you know what will happen; for the man will not rest until he has settled this today."

Chapter 3 Thoughts to Reflect Upon:

Has God ever asked you to do something that seemed really odd? Would you have followed Naomi's advice in approaching Boaz? What can you do to assist one another? How did you feel after reading this chapter? Did any verse stand out to you specifically?

Verse of the Day: 03/   Date:

_____

_____

_____

Journal/Notes Section-

_____

_____

_____

_____

_____

_____

_____

_____

_____

_____

_____

_____

_____

_____

_____

_____

_____

_____

_____

CHAPTER 4
A BLESSED UNION

B oaz is an honorable man because he holds Ruth in high esteem and wants nothing less than for her to become his wife. He is proud to declare this fact in front of the elders. He is redeeming Ruth by proclaiming his interest in her and his intention to proceed with the marriage. But there is one obstacle: another relative in line before him has the first option.

So, first thing in the morning, Boaz calls for a meeting to discuss the matter with the elders. It is interesting how there were ten elders, and we have Ten Commandments given by God. It is almost a metaphor for Christ the Redeemer, not the law.

The closest kinsman could have taken Ruth as his wife. However—much to Boaz's relief—he declines. Possibly her background is unacceptable to him. Or he has already made a commitment. Boaz doesn't care where Ruth comes from: the only thing that matters is this precious jewel he has waited for all his life. So, he purchases everything left for Naomi and pledges to raise up children with Ruth on behalf of the deceased husband.

Finally, we see the redemption of Naomi. God will restore her with a grandson. From a woman marked by bitterness, she returns to her old self, "Naomi the Pleasant." Little Obed sitting in her lap is the one who will rejuvenate her. Little did she know that she would be the blessed mother of the line leading to the Messiah. What a wonderful example of how God can redeem all of us! Sometimes we can all feel like Naomi, that life has turned bitter, but if we stay faithful to God's commandments, even our most bitter times will end with us smiling. The Bible says that if we delight ourselves in Him, He will give us our heart's desire and more than we can imagine!

Chapter 4 ends by telling us about the ancestry of King David, starting from Perez. It looks like a long list of names that one tends to skip over—that is, until you look closer. Who was Perez, and who was Salmon? Let's turn to Matthew 1:2-6 for a fuller account:

"²Abraham became the father of Isaac. Isaac became the father of Jacob. Jacob became the father of Judah and his brothers. ³Judah became the father of Perez and Zerah by Tamar. Perez became the father of Hezron. Hezron became the father of Ram. ⁴Ram became the father of Amminadab. Amminadab became the father of Nahshon. Nahshon became the father of Salmon. ⁵Salmon became the father of Boaz by Rahab. Boaz became the father of Obed by Ruth. Obed became the father of Jesse. ⁶Jesse became the father of King David."

We see here that Perez was the offspring of Judah and Tamar. Interesting! Wasn't Tamar the daughter-in-law of Judah? Yes, we can see from Genesis 38 that it was an incestuous union from which there were twins, Zerah and Perez. Perez, whose name means "breakthrough," pushed through the birthing process to become the firstborn. Breakthrough Perez was an honorable man and overcame the stigma of his birth.

Now, look at another figure, Salmon. The Matthew account tells us that Salmon was the father of Boaz by Rehab. Do you recognize Rehab, the harlot of Jericho (Joshua 2)? Having sheltered the two spies, she had asked for protection, and she and her family were saved during the fall of Jericho. Many scholars have gone so far as to show that Salmon was, in fact, one of the two spies who then married Rehab.

The point I believe is being made in Matthew 1 is that Jesus' family tree would appear to be tainted by scandals. How shocking! But that is only if you have a religious mindset. The Word of God truly tests our hearts, doesn't it? What comes through in all this disclosure is that God's grace and redemptive power are sufficient to bring cleansing to any bloodline, for we have all sinned and come short. That is why even a Moabite like Ruth can be accepted in the assembly, because she has made Yahweh her Lord. It's all about grace, my friends.

Ruth Chapter 4 Scripture

The Marriage between Boaz and Ruth

1Now Boaz went up to the gate and sat down there. Behold, the near kinsman of whom Boaz spoke came by. Boaz said to him, "Come over here, friend, and sit down!" He came over, and sat down.

2 Boaz took ten men of the elders of the city, and said, "Sit down here," and they sat down.

3 He said to the near kinsman, "Naomi, who has come back out of the country of Moab, is selling the parcel of land, which was our brother Elimelech's.

4 I thought I should tell you, saying, 'Buy it before those who sit here, and before the elders of my people.' If you will redeem it, redeem it; but if you will not redeem it, then tell me, that I may know. For there is no one to redeem it besides you; and I am after you."

He said, "I will redeem it."

5 Then Boaz said, "On the day you buy the field from the hand of Naomi, you must buy it also from Ruth the Moabitess, the wife of the dead, to raise up the name of the dead on his inheritance."

6 The near kinsman said, "I can't redeem it for myself, lest I endanger my own inheritance. Take my right of redemption for yourself; for I can't redeem it."

7 Now this was the custom in former time in Israel concerning redeeming and concerning exchanging, to confirm all things: a man took off his sandal, and gave it to his neighbor; and this was the way of formalizing transactions in Israel.

8 So the near kinsman said to Boaz, "Buy it for yourself," then he took off his sandal.

9 Boaz said to the elders and to all the people, "You are witnesses today, that I have bought all that was Elimelech's, and all that was Chilion's and Mahlon's, from the hand of Naomi.

10 Moreover, Ruth the Moabitess, the wife of Mahlon, I have purchased to be my wife, to raise up the name of the dead on his inheritance, that the name of the dead may not be cut off from among his brothers and from the gate of his place. You are witnesses today."

11 All the people who were in the gate, and the elders, said, "We are witnesses. May Yahweh make the woman who has come into your house like Rachel and like Leah, which both built the house of Israel; and treat you worthily in Ephrathah, and be famous in Bethlehem.

12 Let your house be like the house of Perez, whom Tamar bore to Judah, of the offspring which Yahweh will give you by this young woman."

Through Ruth Naomi Gains a Son

13 So Boaz took Ruth and she became his wife; and he went in to her, and Yahweh enabled her to conceive, and she bore a son.

14 The women said to Naomi, "Blessed be Yahweh, who has not left you today without a near kinsman. Let his name be famous in Israel.

15 He shall be to you a restorer of life and sustain you in your old age; for your daughter-in-law, who loves you, who is better to you than seven sons, has given birth to him."

16 Naomi took the child, laid him in her bosom, and became nurse to him.

17 The women, her neighbors, gave him a name, saying, "A son is born to Naomi". They named him Obed. He is the father of Jesse, the father of David.

The Genealogy of King David

18 Now this is the history of the generations of Perez: Perez became the father of Hezron,

19 and Hezron became the father of Ram, and Ram became the father of Amminadab,

20 and Amminadab became the father of Nahshon, and Nahshon became the father of Salmon,

21 and Salmon became the father of Boaz, and Boaz became the father of Obed,

22 and Obed became the father of Jesse, and Jesse became the father of David.

Chapter 4 Thoughts to Reflect Upon:

Do you believe God redeems? Have you experienced God's restoration? How can the law and God's word redeem you? How did you feel after reading this chapter? Did any verse stand out to you specifically?

Verse of the Day: 04/   Date:

_____

_____

_____

Journal/Notes Section-

_____
_____
_____
_____
_____
_____
_____
_____
_____
_____
_____
_____
_____
_____
_____
_____
_____
_____
_____
_____

CONCLUSION

Redemption is freely offered to anyone who seeks the Lord. The story of Ruth is a clear representation of how Christ redeems us, even when the circumstances go against us or even when we have taken the wrong path. His guiding hand leads us back to Him and the destiny He has called us to—something far more significant than we can imagine. But we must do our part and follow His leading. As Christians, we are also called to lift up the downcast of our society. Let's also be friends with the person at work and seek their interests before ours. The story of Ruth shows us powerful and relevant examples of all these things. We would be wise to follow her precedent.

Outline of Ruth's Ancestors in the Bible

Abraham:

"Terah lived seventy years, and became the father of Abram, Nahor, and Haran. Now this is the history of the generations of Terah. Terah became the father of Abram, Nahor, and Haran. Haran became the father of Lot. Haran died in the land of his birth, in Ur of the Chaldees, while his father Terah was still alive. Abram and Nahor married wives. The name of Abram's wife was Sarai, and the name of Nahor's wife was Milcah, the daughter of Haran, who was also the father of Iscah. Sarai was barren. She had no child. Terah took Abram his son, Lot the son of Haran, his son's son, and Sarai his daughter-in-law, his son Abram's wife. They went from Ur of the Chaldees, to go into the land of Canaan. They came to Haran and lived there. The days of Terah were two hundred five years. Terah died in Haran" (Genesis 11:26-31).

"The book of the genealogy of Jesus Christ, the son of David, the son of Abraham. Abraham became the father of Isaac. Isaac became the father of Jacob. Jacob became the father of Judah and his brothers" (Matthew 1:1-2).

Judah:

"Laban gave Bilhah, his servant, to his daughter Rachel to be her servant. He went in also to Rachel, and he loved also Rachel more than Leah, and served with him seven more years. Yahweh saw that Leah was hated, and he opened her womb, but Rachel was barren. Leah conceived, and bore a son, and she named him Reuben. For she said, "Because Yahweh has looked at my affliction; for now my husband will love me." She conceived again, and bore a son, and said, "Because Yahweh has heard that I am hated, he has therefore given me this son also." She named him Simeon. She conceived again, and bore a son. She said, "Now this time my husband will be joined to me, because I have borne him three sons." Therefore his name was called Levi. She conceived again, and bore a son. She said, "This time I will praise Yahweh." Therefore she named him Judah. Then she stopped bearing" (Genesis 29:29-35).

"The book of the genealogy of Jesus Christ, the son of David, the son of Abraham. Abraham became the father of Isaac. Isaac became the father of Jacob. Jacob became the father of Judah and his brothers" (Matthew 1:1-2).

Perez:

"Now this is the history of the generations of Perez: Perez became the father of Hezron..." (Ruth 4:18).

"Judah became the father of Perez and Zerah by Tamar. Perez became the father of Hezron. Hezron became the father of Ram" (Matthew 1:3).

Boaz:

"Now this is the history of the generations of Perez: Perez became the father of Hezron, and Hezron became the father of Ram, and Ram became the father of Amminadab, and Amminadab became the father of Nahshon, and Nahshon became the father of Salmon, and

Salmon became the father of Boaz, and Boaz became the father of Obed, and Obed became the father of Jesse, and Jesse became the father of David" (Ruth 18-22).

"Salmon became the father of Boaz by Rahab. Boaz became the father of Obed by Ruth. Obed became the father of Jesse" (Matthew 1:5).

Lot:

"Now this is the history of the generations of Terah. Terah became the father of Abram, Nahor, and Haran. Haran became the father of Lot" (Genesis 11:27).

Moab:

"They made their father drink wine that night: and the firstborn went in, and lay with her father. He didn't know when she lay down, nor when she arose. It came to pass on the next day, that the firstborn said to the younger, "Behold, I lay last night with my father. Let's make him drink wine again tonight. You go in, and lie with him, that we may preserve our father's family line." They made their father drink wine that night also. The younger went and lay with him. He didn't know when she lay down, nor when she got up. Thus both of Lot's daughters were with child by their father. The firstborn bore a son, and named him Moab. He is the father of the Moabites to this day" (Genesis 19: 33-37).

Ruth:

"So Boaz took Ruth and she became his wife; and he went in to her, and Yahweh enabled her to conceive, and she bore a son" (Ruth 4:13).

Ruth's Direct Descendants:

Obed/Jesse/David:

"The women, her neighbors, gave him a name, saying, "A son is born to Naomi". They named him Obed. He is the father of Jesse, the father of David" (Ruth 4:17).

"Salmon became the father of Boaz by Rahab. Boaz became the father of Obed by Ruth. Obed became the father of Jesse. Jesse became the father of King David. David became the father of Solomon by her who had been Uriah's wife" (Matthew 1:5-6).

Jesus Christ "the Messiah"

"The book of the genealogy of Jesus Christ, the son of David, the son of Abraham. Abraham became the father of Isaac. Isaac became the father of Jacob. Jacob became the father of Judah and his brothers. Judah became the father of Perez and Zerah by Tamar. Perez became the father of Hezron. Hezron became the father of Ram. Ram became the father of Amminadab. Amminadab became the father of Nahshon. Nahshon became the father of Salmon. Salmon became the father of Boaz by Rahab. Boaz became the father of Obed by Ruth. Obed became the father of Jesse. Jesse became the father of King David. David became the father of Solomon by her who had been Uriah's wife. Solomon became the father of Rehoboam. Rehoboam became the father of Abijah. Abijah became the father of Asa. Asa became the father of Jehoshaphat. Jehoshaphat became the father of Joram. Joram became the father of Uzziah. Uzziah became the father of Jotham. Jotham became the father of Ahaz. Ahaz became the father of Hezekiah. Hezekiah became the father of Manasseh. Manasseh became the father of Amon. Amon became the father of Josiah. Josiah became the father of Jechoniah and his brothers at the time of the exile to Babylon.

"After the exile to Babylon, Jechoniah became the father of Shealtiel. Shealtiel became the father of Zerubbabel. Zerubbabel became the father of Abiud. Abiud became the father of Eliakim. Eliakim became the father of Azor. Azor became the father of Zadok. Zadok became the father of Achim. Achim became the father of Eliud. Eliud became the father of Eleazar. Eleazar became the father of Matthan. Matthan became the father of Jacob. Jacob became the father of Joseph, the husband of Mary, from whom was born Jesus, who is called Christ.

So all the generations from Abraham to David are fourteen generations; from David to the exile to Babylon fourteen generations; and from the carrying away to Babylon to the Christ, fourteen generations. Now the birth of Jesus Christ was like this: After his mother, Mary, was engaged to Joseph, before they came together, she was found pregnant by the Holy Spirit" (Matthew 1:1-18).

"Therefore the Lord himself will give you a sign. Behold, the virgin will conceive, and bear a son, and shall call his name Immanuel" (Isaiah 7:14).

THE BOOK OF ESTHER

ABOUT THE BOOK OF ESTHER

This story takes place in Persia, far away from the Promised Land. Many Jews lived there because their families had been taken captive during the reign of King Nebuchadnezzar and brought to Babylon, which later became Persia. There is no mention of God in the book, yet the story clearly reveals God's sovereignty over the lives of His people. He places His loving hand over us to guide our steps and deliver us from every evil circumstance.

The two main characters, Esther and Mordecai, were no different than you and me. Esther was an orphan gifted with extraordinary beauty, and we see her developing into a woman of great strength and wisdom to meet tremendous challenges. She was raised by her cousin Mordecai, a man of loyalty, great integrity, and devotion to God. Christians all over the world also live "in exile" in a society that does not know God, yet the story of Esther displays how God will redeem His people. We must trust that the Lord has a plan to save His people wherever they are placed.

This story of Esther and Mordecai is something we can all relate to, and it makes the Book of Esther one that can breathe new life into our faith. After all, faith is all about trusting God, and Esther shows us precisely how to do that. Her trust in God and in His plan helps her overcome seemingly insurmountable odds. At the end of the day, her people are saved, and she is allowed to be part of God's glorious plan, all because she trusted in Him.

There will be times in life when we, too, will face circumstances that seem impossible for us to conquer. In those times, we must not be afraid. We must remember that God is stronger than anything we face. When we walk with Him, He shares His power with us, just like He did with Esther so long ago. With God by our side, we can accomplish anything He has called us to do! The story of Esther is a powerful demonstration of that.

CHAPTER 1
A FEAST THAT CHANGED DESTINIES

How fun it is to have a feast for so many days! Honestly, I would be very merry with an opportunity to eat all I wanted for 180 days if I were one of the king's servants. I would be partying for seven days straight if I were a regular civilian. It sounds like a fun kingdom to be in. This was the kingdom King Ahasuerus inherited from his father. Archeologists have found the exact ruins of where the events took place.

Now the story gets interesting. As the king gets "merry with wine," he loses self-control and starts to brag. He calls for his beautiful wife Vashti to display herself to his guests. Although there is no indication in the chapter, we can assume she was asked to expose herself indecently, perhaps strip or be provocative in some way. It is unclear why she didn't comply, but it could be that she wanted to keep her modesty. At any rate, she was holding her own private banquet with her ladies at the time.

Clearly, this husband did not love his wife the way God intended. If he did, he wouldn't have asked her to make a mockery of her body and herself. Vashti's refusal was a public affront to the king. Unfortunately, this put her at significant risk, for the king's command was absolute. History reveals King Ahasuerus as a foolish and impulsive man who relied on his counselors' advice. His counselors feared that the queen's disobedience would set a precedent for other women in the kingdom. Therefore, on their advice, the king had Queen Vashti dethroned and evicted from the palace.

It is clear his wife had no respect for him either. A man can force his wife into submission but may never gain her respect. Vashti had every right to refuse to engage in any kind of sinful behavior. What is the point of marriage if your character causes your wife to disrespect you? Why be married if you can't respect your spouse either?

Husbands, you have an important role. In loving your wife as your own flesh, you are demonstrating the love of Christ for His own people.

"Husbands, love your wives, even as Christ also loved the assembly, and gave himself up for it; that he might sanctify it, having cleansed it by the washing of water with the word, that he might present the assembly to himself gloriously, not having spot or wrinkle or any such thing; but that it should be holy and without defect. Even so husbands also ought to love their own wives as their own bodies. He who loves his own wife loves himself. For no man ever hated his own flesh; but nourishes and cherishes it, even as the Lord also does the assembly; because we are members of his body, of his flesh and bones." (Ephesians 5:25-30)

Esther Chapter 1 Scripture

King Ahasuerus Prepares a Feast

1 Now in the days of Ahasuerus (this is Ahasuerus who reigned from India even to Ethiopia, over one hundred twenty-seven provinces),

2 in those days, when the King Ahasuerus sat on the throne of his kingdom, which was in Susa the palace,

3 in the third year of his reign, he made a feast for all his princes and his servants; the power of Persia and Media, the nobles and princes of the provinces, being before him.

4 He displayed the riches of his glorious kingdom and the honor of his excellent majesty many days, even one hundred eighty days.

5 When these days were fulfilled, the king made a seven day feast for all the people who were present in Susa the palace, both great and small, in the court of the garden of the king's palace.

6 There were hangings of white and blue material, fastened with cords of fine linen and purple to silver rings and marble pillars. The couches were of gold and silver, on a pavement of red, white, yellow, and black marble.

7 They gave them drinks in golden vessels of various kinds, including royal wine in abundance, according to the bounty of the king.

8 In accordance with the law, the drinking was not compulsory; for so the king had instructed all the officials of his house, that they should do according to every man's pleasure.

9 Also Vashti the queen made a feast for the women in the royal house which belonged to King Ahasuerus.

Queen Vashti Dethroned

10 On the seventh day, when the heart of the king was merry with wine, he commanded Mehuman, Biztha, Harbona, Bigtha, and Abagtha, Zethar, and Carcass, the seven eunuchs who served in the presence of Ahasuerus the king,

11 to bring Vashti the queen before the king with the royal crown, to show the people and the princes her beauty; for she was beautiful.

12 But the queen Vashti refused to come at the king's commandment by the eunuchs. Therefore the king was very angry, and his anger burned in him.

13 Then the king said to the wise men, who knew the times (for it was the king's custom to consult those who knew law and judgment;

14 and next to him were Carshena, Shethar, Admatha, Tarshish, Meres, Marsena, and Memucan, the seven princes of Persia and Media, who saw the king's face, and sat first in the kingdom),

15 "What shall we do to Queen Vashti according to law, because she has not done the bidding of the King Ahasuerus by the eunuchs?"

16 Memucan answered before the king and the princes, "Vashti the queen has not done wrong to just the king, but also to all the princes, and to all the people who are in all the provinces of the King Ahasuerus.

17 For this deed of the queen will become known to all women, causing them to show contempt for their husbands, when it is reported, 'King Ahasuerus commanded Vashti the queen to be brought in before him, but she didn't come.'

18 Today, the princesses of Persia and Media who have heard of the queen's deed will tell all the king's princes. This will cause much contempt and wrath.

19 "If it pleases the king, let a royal commandment go from him, and let it be written among the laws of the Persians and the Medes, so that it cannot be altered, that Vashti may never again come before King Ahasuerus; and let the king give her royal estate to another who is better than she.

20 When the king's decree which he shall make is published throughout all his kingdom (for it is great), all the wives will give their husbands honor, both great and small."

21 This advice pleased the king and the princes, and the king did according to the word of Memucan:

22 for he sent letters into all the king's provinces, into every province according to its writing, and to every people in their language, that every man should rule his own house, speaking in the language of his own people.

Chapter 1 Thoughts to Reflect Upon:

Have you ever been as prideful as the king in any position of authority? Did people only admire you for your looks or status as opposed to your character? How did you feel? Have you ever avoided a situation because it conflicted with God's will or law? Did obeying God, as opposed to man, have any consequences? How did you feel after reading this chapter? Did any verse stand out to you specifically?

Verse of the Day: 01/   Date:

_____

_____

_____

Journal/Notes Section-

_____

_____

_____

_____

_____

_____

_____

_____

_____

_____

_____

_____

_____

_____

_____

_____

_____

CHAPTER 2
ESTHER BECOMES QUEEN

I t seems as if some time has passed since the startling events of chapter 1. King Ahasuerus was a man who loved women. His servants knew this and decided to go and find a young virgin for him to replace the queen. This endeavor is ironic, considering what Ahasuerus wanted his wife, Vashti, to do in front of a leering male audience.

Through the search for a suitable replacement, the king would meet Esther, this beautiful, kindhearted young Jewish virgin. An orphan, she was raised by her cousin Mordecai, who commanded her to keep her Jewish nationality secret. It is unclear why she was told to keep her nationality secret when we would later see Mordecai openly speaking about his Jewish identity. It could be that this might have prejudiced her application to the palace or that she would have been perceived as coming from a lowly family.

Esther would be put with the king's harem, overseen by one of the king's eunuchs, Hegai. A eunuch is a man who has been castrated to safeguard the women in his charge. Esther would immediately gain the favor of Hegai, and he would provide her with all the beauty advice and cosmetics she needed.

Of course, by having so many women, the king is breaking God's law of monogamous marriage. The women are kept locked up, as he chooses which one to take to his bedchamber at his pleasure. Although these events are somewhat troubling, God is setting a series of activities in motion to accomplish a bigger plan. Esther would gain much favor in the eyes of the king and everyone around her. The king would finally place the crown on her head to take Vashti's place, and her status would be elevated above all the other virgins.

"The king's heart is in Yahweh's hand like the watercourses. He turns it wherever he desires (Proverbs 21:1)."

The chapter ends by recounting how Mordecai learns of a plot by two of the king's eunuchs to assassinate the king. He informs Esther, who alerts the king, and the men responsible are hanged. God would use Esther to protect the king so that God could use her to deliver His people later.

Esther Chapter 2 Scripture

Esther Becomes Queen

1 After these things, when the wrath of King Ahasuerus was pacified, he remembered Vashti, and what she had done, and what was decreed against her.

2 Then the king's servants who served him said, "Let beautiful young virgins be sought for the king.

3 Let the king appoint officers in all the provinces of his kingdom, that they may gather together all the beautiful young virgins to the citadel of Susa, to the women's house, to the custody of Hegai the king's eunuch, keeper of the women. Let cosmetics be given them;

4 and let the maiden who pleases the king be queen instead of Vashti." The thing pleased the king, and he did so.

5 There was a certain Jew in the citadel of Susa, whose name was Mordecai, the son of Jair, the son of Shimei, the son of Kish, a Benjamite,

6 who had been carried away from Jerusalem with the captives who had been carried away with Jeconiah king of Judah, whom Nebuchadnezzar the king of Babylon had carried away.

7 He brought up Hadassah, that is, Esther, his uncle's daughter; for she had neither father nor mother. The maiden was fair and beautiful; and when her father and mother were dead, Mordecai took her for his own daughter.

8 So, when the king's commandment and his decree was heard, and when many maidens were gathered together to the citadel of Susa, to the custody of Hegai, Esther was taken into the king's house, to the custody of Hegai, keeper of the women.

9 The maiden pleased him, and she obtained kindness from him. He quickly gave her cosmetics and her portions of food, and the seven choice maidens who were to be given her out of the king's house. He moved her and her maidens to the best place in the women's house.

10 Esther had not made known her people nor her relatives, because Mordecai had instructed her that she should not make it known.

11 Mordecai walked every day in front of the court of the women's house, to find out how Esther was doing, and what would become of her.

12 Each young woman's turn came to go in to King Ahasuerus after her purification for twelve months (for so were the days of their purification accomplished, six months with oil of myrrh, and six months with sweet fragrances and with preparations for beautifying women).

13 The young woman then came to the king like this: whatever she desired was given her to go with her out of the women's house to the king's house.

14 In the evening she went, and on the next day she returned into the second women's house, to the custody of Shaashgaz, the king's eunuch, who kept the concubines. She came in to the king no more, unless the king delighted in her, and she was called by name.

15 Now when the turn of Esther, the daughter of Abihail the uncle of Mordecai, who had taken her for his daughter, came to go in to the king, she required nothing but what Hegai the king's eunuch, the keeper of the women, advised. Esther obtained favor in the sight of all those who looked at her.

16 So Esther was taken to King Ahasuerus into his royal house in the tenth month, which is the month Tebeth, in the seventh year of his reign.

17 The king loved Esther more than all the women, and she obtained favor and kindness in his sight more than all the virgins; so that he set the royal crown on her head, and made her queen instead of Vashti.

18 Then the king made a great feast for all his princes and his servants, even Esther's feast; and he proclaimed a holiday in the provinces, and gave gifts according to the king's bounty.

Mordecai Hears of a Plot against the King

19 When the virgins were gathered together the second time, Mordecai was sitting in the king's gate.

20 Esther had not yet made known her relatives nor her people, as Mordecai had commanded her; for Esther obeyed Mordecai, like she did when she was brought up by him.

21 In those days, while Mordecai was sitting in the king's gate, two of the king's eunuchs, Bigthan and Teresh, who were doorkeepers, were angry, and sought to lay hands on the King Ahasuerus.

22 This thing became known to Mordecai, who informed Esther the queen; and Esther informed the king in Mordecai's name.

23 When this matter was investigated, and it was found to be so, they were both hanged on a gallows; and it was written in the book of the chronicles in the king's presence.

Chapter 2 Thoughts to Reflect Upon:

Have you ever waited for something for a long time? Can you describe how you felt during the long wait? Do you agree that outward purity does not equate with pureness of heart? Check your heart today. Would God have been willing to use anyone for the role of queen, or did He pick the right person? How did you feel after reading this chapter? Did any verse stand out to you specifically?

Verse of the Day: 02/   Date:

_____

_____

_____

Journal/Notes Section-

_____

_____

_____

_____

_____

_____

_____

_____

_____

_____

_____

_____

_____

_____

_____

_____

_____

_____

CHAPTER 3
A VILE PLOT

This chapter has deep intimations of the Holocaust in Nazi Germany. The Jews living amongst the Persians were law-abiding citizens, and there was no reason to expect any conspiracy among them. They must have been shocked at the sudden threat of annihilation due to orders from Haman.

Haman's motives were personal. He was outraged that Mordecai did not bow to him after his promotion by the king. It is scary to think an individual can have so much hatred simply because someone wouldn't acknowledge him. I am thankful not to have an ego as frail as Haman's. But, sadly, there are some in this world who do. Throughout history, we have seen people like this wreak great havoc on whole communities. The Holocaust was one such time, but there were many other calamities in the past as well.

But what's worse is that he transferred that hatred for one man to the entire Jewish nation living in Persia. We note that Haman was a descendant of King Agag of the Amalekites, and this was a warlike tribe with whom the Israelites were engaged for generations. The murderous spirit he carried may have been his motivation to annihilate a whole race of innocent people.

"Yahweh said to Moses, "Write this for a memorial in a book, and rehearse it in the ears of Joshua: that I will utterly blot out the memory of Amalek from under the sky." Moses built an altar, and called its name "Yahweh our Banner". He said, "Yah has sworn: 'Yahweh will have war with Amalek from generation to generation" (Exodus 17:14-16).

When an ungodly man rises to power, it brings fear and ruins the lives of many: "When the righteous thrive, the people rejoice; but when the wicked rule, the people groan (Proverbs 29:2)."

We must pray for those around the world who are living under such frightening regimes. There are still places in the world where people live under the rule of cruel and heartless dictators. We must give them our continued prayers and support in any way we can. They are God's children and deserve to live with peace, hope, and joy.

Esther Chapter 3 Scripture

Haman Conspires to Destroy God's People

1 After these things King Ahasuerus promoted Haman the son of Hammedatha the Agagite, and advanced him, and set his seat above all the princes who were with him.

2 All the king's servants who were in the king's gate bowed down, and paid homage to Haman; for the king had so commanded concerning him. But Mordecai didn't bow down or pay him homage.

3 Then the king's servants, who were in the king's gate, said to Mordecai, "Why do you disobey the king's commandment?"

4 Now it came to pass, when they spoke daily to him, and he didn't listen to them, that they told Haman, to see whether Mordecai's reason would stand; for he had told them that he was a Jew.

5 When Haman saw that Mordecai didn't bow down, nor pay him homage, Haman was full of wrath.

6 But he scorned the thought of laying hands on Mordecai alone, for they had made known to him Mordecai's people. Therefore Haman sought to destroy all the Jews who were throughout the whole kingdom of Ahasuerus, even Mordecai's people.

7 In the first month, which is the month Nisan, in the twelfth year of King Ahasuerus, they cast Pur, that is, the lot, before Haman from day to day, and from month to month, and chose the twelfth month, which is the month Adar.

8 Haman said to King Ahasuerus, "There is a certain people scattered abroad and dispersed among the peoples in all the provinces of your kingdom, and their laws are different from other people's. They don't keep the king's laws. Therefore it is not for the king's profit to allow them to remain.

9 If it pleases the king, let it be written that they be destroyed; and I will pay ten thousand talents of silver into the hands of those who are in charge of the king's business, to bring it into the king's treasuries."

10 The king took his ring from his hand, and gave it to Haman the son of Hammedatha the Agagite, the Jews' enemy.

11 The king said to Haman, "The silver is given to you, the people also, to do with them as it seems good to you."

12 Then the king's scribes were called in on the first month, on the thirteenth day of the month; and all that Haman commanded was written to the king's local governors, and to the governors who were over every province, and to the princes of every people, to every province according to its writing, and to every people in their language. It was written in the name of King Ahasuerus, and it was sealed with the king's ring.

13 Letters were sent by couriers into all the king's provinces, to destroy, to kill, and to cause to perish, all Jews, both young and old, little children and women, in one day, even on the thirteenth day of

the twelfth month, which is the month Adar, and to plunder their possessions.

14 A copy of the letter, that the decree should be given out in every province, was published to all the peoples, that they should be ready against that day.

15 The couriers went out in haste by the king's commandment, and the decree was given out in the citadel of Susa. The king and Haman sat down to drink; but the city of Susa was perplexed.

Chapter 3 Thoughts to Reflect Upon:

Haman was a prideful man. Is there a Haman in you? Would you obey God or would you obey Haman if you were offended? Describe a time you felt jealous and how God worked this out. Can you recall a time when someone helped you? How did you feel after reading this chapter? Did any verse stand out to you specifically?

Verse of the Day: 03/   Date:

_____

_____

_____

Journal/Notes Section-

_____

_____

_____

_____

_____

_____

_____

_____

_____

_____

_____

_____

_____

_____

_____

_____

_____

_____

_____

CHAPTER 4
A MOMENTOUS DECISION

This chapter contains the famous line "for such a time as this." Here we see Mordecai refusing to live in any kind of comfort while his people are suffering, and he throws in his lot with his fellow Jews. What a fascinating display of integrity; this man refused clothing from Esther and continued to trust God to deliver His people!

In life, we will enter dark places, sometimes unexpectedly. Uncomfortable and upset as we are, we must remember that we are here by God's will. If God willed us to be somewhere else, we would be there. Let us not focus on where we prefer to be when God has placed us in our current situation for a divine purpose. Let us choose to be aligned with God's purpose by surrendering everything and placing Yahweh first.

"You shall love Yahweh your God with all your heart, with all your soul, and with all your might" (Deuteronomy 6:5).

Esther was unaware of all the trials happening to her people until her eunuchs and maids broke Mordecai's news. Mordecai now insists she intercede on behalf of the Jewish nation.

We now see Esther in a tricky situation. She has not seen her husband, the king, for thirty days. Most likely, he was taking his delight in other young women, too preoccupied to concern himself with the problems of the woman he had made his wife. Her main reasoning was that no one was allowed to enter the king's presence unless summoned by the king. Unless he held out the golden scepter, the penalty for such intrusion was death.

Afraid for her own life, she argued with Mordecai about her role in this. Right, everybody has frightening moments, even the queen. But Mordecai's rebuke goes to the heart of the matter: "Don't think to yourself that you will escape in the king's house any more than all the Jews. For if you remain silent now, then relief and deliverance will come to the Jews from another place, but you and your father's house will perish. **Who knows if you haven't come to the kingdom for such a time as this**?" (Esther 4:13-14, emphasis added)

Those words really impact a tender girl who has no experience in fighting. Now she rises to her full stature as queen because she believes that God gave her the status for a reason. She says: "Go, gather together all the Jews who are present in Susa, and fast for me, and neither eat nor drink three days, night or day. I and my maidens will also fast the same way. Then I will go in to the king, which is against the law; and **if I perish, I perish**" (Esther 4:16, emphasis added).

How brave she is! She was able to conquer her fear via prayers, and her devotion to her people is to the point of giving up her life for them. This sacrifice is a testimony of how our lives should be as we follow Jesus and godly principles with everything we have to the point of unfavorable circumstances or even death. Regardless of the outcome, let us stay God's course for us.

Esther Chapter 4 Scripture

Esther is Informed of Haman's Plans

1 Now when Mordecai found out all that was done, Mordecai tore his clothes, and put on sackcloth with ashes, and went out into the middle of the city, and wailed loudly and bitterly.

2 He came even before the king's gate, for no one is allowed inside the king's gate clothed with sackcloth.

3 In every province, wherever the king's commandment and his decree came, there was great mourning among the Jews, and fasting, and weeping, and wailing; and many lay in sackcloth and ashes.

4 Esther's maidens and her eunuchs came and told her this, and the queen was exceedingly grieved. She sent clothing to Mordecai, to replace his sackcloth; but he didn't receive it.

5 Then Esther called for Hathach, one of the king's eunuchs, whom he had appointed to attend her, and commanded him to go to Mordecai, to find out what this was, and why it was.

6 So Hathach went out to Mordecai, to city square which was before the king's gate.

7 Mordecai told him of all that had happened to him, and the exact sum of the money that Haman had promised to pay to the king's treasuries for the destruction of the Jews.

8 He also gave him the copy of the writing of the decree that was given out in Susa to destroy them, to show it to Esther, and to declare it to her, and to urge her to go in to the king, to make supplication to him, and to make request before him, for her people.

9 Hathach came and told Esther the words of Mordecai.

10 Then Esther spoke to Hathach, and gave him a message to Mordecai:

11 "All the king's servants and the people of the king's provinces know that whoever, whether man or woman, comes to the king into the inner court without being called, there is one law for him, that he be put to death, except those to whom the king might hold out the golden scepter, that he may live. I have not been called to come in to the king these thirty days."

12 They told Esther's words to Mordecai.

13 Then Mordecai asked them to return this answer to Esther: "Don't think to yourself that you will escape in the king's house any more than all the Jews.

14 For if you remain silent now, then relief and deliverance will come to the Jews from another place, but you and your father's house will perish. Who knows if you haven't come to the kingdom for such a time as this?"

15 Then Esther asked them to answer Mordecai,

16 "Go, gather together all the Jews who are present in Susa, and fast for me, and neither eat nor drink three days, night or day. I and my maidens will also fast the same way. Then I will go in to the king, which is against the law; and if I perish, I perish."

17 So Mordecai went his way, and did according to all that Esther had commanded him.

Chapter 4 Thoughts to Reflect Upon:

We are living sacrifices to our God; are you willing to sacrifice your life? Has God ever placed you in a situation where you had a specific purpose? Do you consult God before taking a major step? Do you feel you are irreplaceable? How did you feel after reading this chapter? Did any verse stand out to you specifically?

Verse of the Day: 04/   Date:

_____

_____

_____

Journal/Notes Section-

_____

_____

_____

_____

_____

_____

_____

_____

_____

_____

_____

_____

_____

_____

_____

_____

_____

_____

CHAPTER 5
INVITATION TO A BANQUET

P icture yourself in a gown befitting a queen. After you fast, you now have the clarity and courage to approach your husband, who happens to be the king. It's been over thirty days since you last saw each other, and you pray within yourself, knowing this could very well be your last day on earth.

Esther was well aware that anyone who approached the king without his consent would be placing their life on the line. What a relief when the king, seeing Esther standing in the palace court in her royal robes, held up his golden scepter, signaling that her life was spared! He was attentive to her and said he would give her whatever she requested. God had indeed placed Esther in this strategic position "for such a time as this."

Esther was full of wisdom as she worked out her next move. Rather than simply blurting out to the king all about the plot, she acted calmly. Favor was required first. She simply invited the king and Haman to be her guests at a banquet she would have for two days. There was no hint of anything suspicious!

When Haman heard he had been invited to a special banquet, he was puffed up with pride, oblivious of the trap. He boasted of all his achievements to his wife and friends. However, one thing that pained him was that Mordecai still refused to acknowledge his status. This one thing irked him despite his wealth, power, and titles. So, on his wife's and friends' advice, he decided to use this opportunity at the banquet to get the king's permission to have Mordecai hanged.

Esther Chapter 5 Scripture

Esther Risks Her Life to Make an Appeal to King Ahasuerus

1 Now on the third day, Esther put on her royal clothing, and stood in the inner court of the king's house, next to the king's house. The king sat on his royal throne in the royal house, next to the entrance of the house.

2 When the king saw Esther the queen standing in the court, she obtained favor in his sight; and the king held out to Esther the golden scepter that was in his hand. So Esther came near, and touched the top of the scepter.

3 Then the king asked her, "What would you like, queen Esther? What is your request? It shall be given you even to the half of the kingdom."

4 Esther said, "If it seems good to the king, let the king and Haman come today to the banquet that I have prepared for him."

5 Then the king said, "Bring Haman quickly, so that it may be done as Esther has said." So the king and Haman came to the banquet that Esther had prepared.

6 The king said to Esther at the banquet of wine, "What is your petition? It shall be granted you. What is your request? Even to the half of the kingdom it shall be performed."

7 Then Esther answered and said, "My petition and my request is this.

8 If I have found favor in the sight of the king, and if it pleases the king to grant my petition and to perform my request, let the king and

Haman come to the banquet that I will prepare for them, and I will do tomorrow as the king has said."

Haman Displays Hatred for Mordecai

9 Then Haman went out that day joyful and glad of heart, but when Haman saw Mordecai in the king's gate, that he didn't stand up nor move for him, he was filled with wrath against Mordecai.

10 Nevertheless Haman restrained himself, and went home. There, he sent and called for his friends and Zeresh his wife.

11 Haman recounted to them the glory of his riches, the multitude of his children, all the things in which the king had promoted him, and how he had advanced him above the princes and servants of the king.

12 Haman also said, "Yes, Esther the queen let no man come in with the king to the banquet that she had prepared but myself; and tomorrow I am also invited by her together with the king.

13 Yet all this avails me nothing, so long as I see Mordecai the Jew sitting at the king's gate."

14 Then Zeresh his wife and all his friends said to him, "Let a gallows be made fifty cubits high, and in the morning speak to the king about hanging Mordecai on it. Then go in merrily with the king to the banquet." This pleased Haman, so he had the gallows made.

Chapter 5 Thoughts to Reflect Upon:

How often do you fast? Do you make your request known to God? Do you come to Him with fasting to offer your body as a living sacrifice? Describe a time you used wisdom to be patient and tactful about a response. Just as Esther was wise at this moment, are you also wise in your dealings? How did you feel after reading this chapter? Did any verse stand out to you specifically?

Verse of the Day: 05/   Date:

_____

_____

_____

Journal/Notes Section-

_____

_____

_____

_____

_____

_____

_____

_____

_____

_____

_____

_____

_____

_____

_____

_____

_____

_____

CHAPTER 6
RECOGNITION FOR MORDECAI

I t's difficult to sleep when we have things on our minds. Sometimes God keeps us awake for a purpose. We see how God made the king restless that night and placed it on his heart to recall the book of records. Of all the bedtime stories, why the book of records?

It was God who ordered his footsteps. Any book from the record of chronicles could have been brought, any page read, but only what God wanted the king to remember was read: the account of how Mordecai saved him from the assassins. It is interesting to see so many "coincidences" in this chapter. We know God is ultimately in control, and nothing happens by accident.

As a result, the king wished to reward Mordecai and sought Haman's advice on how he should honor a man he delighted in. Pridefully thinking such honor was meant for him, Haman recommended a public proclamation of such a man as he rode on horseback through the city; what a shock to discover that the man was Mordecai and what humiliation to have to be the one to make the proclamation! This event is the beginning of the end for Haman, as his wife rightfully observed. For if the one being honored was a Jew, it would not go well for the one who planned the downfall of this community.

The chapter ends with Haman being escorted to the banquet which Queen Esther has prepared. The story's antagonist is being set up to receive what he rightfully deserves. God always rewards the righteous and punishes the wicked.

Sometimes in life, it may seem as if the wicked and unjust are prevailing, while the righteous suffer. In these times, we must cling to God's promises. This story is the perfect reminder that, even when it isn't immediately apparent, the wicked person's actions lead them to ruin. Even though we must be patient, God will reward our righteousness when the time comes. In the meantime, He gives us everything we need to endure the trials we may be facing. All the while, we can rest assured that His plans will ultimately come to fruition.

Esther Chapter 6 Scripture

Mordecai's Loyalty is Remembered

1 On that night, the king couldn't sleep. He commanded the book of records of the chronicles to be brought, and they were read to the king.

2 It was found written that Mordecai had told of Bigthana and Teresh, two of the king's eunuchs, who were doorkeepers, who had tried to lay hands on the King Ahasuerus.

3 The king said, "What honor and dignity has been given to Mordecai for this?"

Then the king's servants who attended him said, "Nothing has been done for him."

4 The king said, "Who is in the court?" Now Haman had come into the outer court of the king's house, to speak to the king about hanging Mordecai on the gallows that he had prepared for him.

5 The king's servants said to him, "Behold, Haman stands in the court." The king said, "Let him come in."

6 So Haman came in. The king said to him, "What shall be done to the man whom the king delights to honor?"

Now Haman said in his heart, "Who would the king delight to honor more than myself?"

7 Haman said to the king, "For the man whom the king delights to honor,

8 let royal clothing be brought which the king uses to wear, and the horse that the king rides on, and on the head of which a royal crown is set.

9 Let the clothing and the horse be delivered to the hand of one of the king's most noble princes, that they may array the man whom the king delights to honor with them, and have him ride on horseback through the city square, and proclaim before him, 'Thus it shall be done to the man whom the king delights to honor!'"

10 Then the king said to Haman, "Hurry and take the clothing and the horse, as you have said, and do this for Mordecai the Jew, who sits at the king's gate. Let nothing fail of all that you have spoken."

11 Then Haman took the clothing and the horse, and arrayed Mordecai, and had him ride through the city square, and proclaimed before him, "Thus it shall be done to the man whom the king delights to honor!"

12 Mordecai came back to the king's gate, but Haman hurried to his house, mourning and having his head covered.

13 Haman recounted to Zeresh his wife and all his friends everything that had happened to him. Then his wise men and Zeresh his wife said to him, "If Mordecai, before whom you have begun to fall, is of Jewish descent, you will not prevail against him, but you will surely fall before him."

14 While they were yet talking with him, the king's eunuchs came, and hurried to bring Haman to the banquet that Esther had prepared.

Chapter 6 Thoughts to Reflect Upon:

Have you had the experience of staring at the ceiling and couldn't fall asleep? Has God ever worked on your thoughts on a sleepless night like that? Have you ever found a God-given coincidence? How did you handle it? Do you believe you are righteous enough for God to hear your prayers? What would you have done in this situation? How did you feel after reading this chapter? Did any verse stand out to you specifically?

Verse of the Day: 06/   Date:

_____

_____

_____

Journal/Notes Section-

_____

_____

_____

_____

_____

_____

_____

_____

_____

_____

_____

_____

_____

_____

CHAPTER 7
HAMAN EXPOSED

Day two of the banquet set the stage for justice to be served on Haman. The king publicly proclaimed he would give Esther anything she wanted—up to half of his kingdom. Esther, being a righteous woman, wanted nothing more than the lives of herself and her people to be spared. Great diplomacy is seen in the way she made her petition to the king.

When Esther revealed the truth that Haman was the adversary, the king was so enraged he had to step outside to collect his thoughts. It was customary for people to sit or lie during drinking or eating, and Haman adopted such a posture before Esther to plead for his life. As he was in this supplicating posture, the king came in and at once interpreted this act as an assault on the queen right there in front of him.

The gallows prepared for Mordecai were the gallows on which Haman was hanged. "Whoever digs a pit shall fall into it," says Proverbs 26:27. Justice was served, and the king's wrath was appeased. Here we see God's faithfulness to His promises. God delivers justice to the wicked and gives victory to the righteous. If we walk in God's love and truth, we will walk in the path of the righteous instead of being pulled away by the wicked. And at the end of that path is an eternity in God's presence.

Esther Chapter 7 Scripture

Esther Makes Her Petition

1 So the king and Haman came to banquet with Esther the queen.

2 The king said again to Esther on the second day at the banquet of wine, "What is your petition, queen Esther? It shall be granted you. What is your request? Even to the half of the kingdom it shall be performed."

3 Then Esther the queen answered, "If I have found favor in your sight, O king, and if it pleases the king, let my life be given me at my petition, and my people at my request.

4 For we are sold, I and my people, to be destroyed, to be slain, and to perish. But if we had been sold for male and female slaves, I would have held my peace, although the adversary could not have compensated for the king's loss."

5 Then King Ahasuerus said to Esther the queen, "Who is he, and where is he who dared presume in his heart to do so?"

6 Esther said, "An adversary and an enemy, even this wicked Haman!" Then Haman was afraid before the king and the queen.

7 The king arose in his wrath from the banquet of wine and went into the palace garden. Haman stood up to make request for his life to Esther the queen; for he saw that there was evil determined against him by the king.

8 Then the king returned out of the palace garden into the place of the banquet of wine; and Haman had fallen on the couch where Esther was. Then the king said, "Will he even assault the queen in front of me in the house?" As the word went out of the king's mouth, they covered Haman's face.

Haman Hanged Instead of Mordecai

9 Then Harbonah, one of the eunuchs who were with the king said, "Behold, the gallows fifty cubits high, which Haman has made for Mordecai, who spoke good for the king, is standing at Haman's house."

The king said, "Hang him on it!"

10 So they hanged Haman on the gallows that he had prepared for Mordecai. Then the king's wrath was pacified.

Chapter 7 Thoughts to Reflect Upon:

Have you ever had to ask God for the right words to say when someone attacked you? Have you ever found yourself to be extremely angry? How did you handle it? Did someone manipulate you into harming another? Have you noticed that when we try to hurt others, we end up hurting ourselves? How did you feel after that? Do you think God cares about your past or your future? How did you feel after reading this chapter? Did any verse stand out to you specifically?

Verse of the Day: 07/   Date:

_____

_____

_____

Journal/Notes Section-

_____

_____

_____

_____

_____

_____

_____

_____

CHAPTER 8
STAND UP AND FIGHT!

Haman had achieved everything a man could want. Now he was dead, and his legacy was gone. Everything Haman possessed, including his ring, estate, and position, was now in Mordecai's hands. While Haman's life ended in disgrace, Mordecai was exalted.

The wages of sin is death. Let us be wary of pride and self-promotion, which leads to greed and covetousness.

So as Mordecai, Esther, and the Jews prayed, fasted, and trusted for the Lord to deliver them, God came through remarkably. There was only one difficulty: the king's decree against the Jews still stood, and, according to Persian law, it could not be revoked. All the same, Esther pleaded with the king, and a way was found to mitigate the first decree by instituting a second decree that allowed people of Jewish origin to defend themselves when attacked.

"In those letters, the king granted the Jews who were in every city to gather themselves together, and to defend their life, to destroy, to kill, and to cause to perish, all the power of the people and province that would assault them, their little ones and women, and to plunder their possessions on one day in all the provinces of King Ahasuerus, on the thirteenth day of the twelfth month, which is the month Adar" (Esther 8:11-12).

Getting the word out was a vast undertaking because of the kingdom's size, and it would take several months to reach all the provinces. Nevertheless, it was done and was enacted. The people now had "light, gladness, and honor." They trusted in their king yet again. Not only were their lives saved, but the people could defend themselves with dignity. Such was the terror they presented to their attackers that many inhabitants of the land "became Jews; for fear of the Jews had fallen on them" (Esther 8:17).

Esther Chapter 8 Scripture

A Decree by the King is Passed on Behalf of the Jews

1 On that day, King Ahasuerus gave the house of Haman, the Jews' enemy, to Esther the queen. Mordecai came before the king; for Esther had told what he was to her.

2 The king took off his ring, which he had taken from Haman, and gave it to Mordecai. Esther set Mordecai over the house of Haman.

3 Esther spoke yet again before the king, and fell down at his feet, and begged him with tears to put away the mischief of Haman the Agagite, and his plan that he had planned against the Jews.

4 Then the king held out to Esther the golden scepter. So Esther arose, and stood before the king.

5 She said, "If it pleases the king, and if I have found favor in his sight, and the thing seems right to the king, and I am pleasing in his eyes, let it be written to reverse the letters devised by Haman, the son of Hammedatha the Agagite, which he wrote to destroy the Jews who are in all the king's provinces.

6 For how can I endure to see the evil that would come to my people? How can I endure to see the destruction of my relatives?"

7 Then King Ahasuerus said to Esther the queen and to Mordecai the Jew, "See, I have given Esther the house of Haman, and they have hanged him on the gallows, because he laid his hand on the Jews.

8 Write also to the Jews, as it pleases you, in the king's name, and seal it with the king's ring; for the writing which is written in the king's name, and sealed with the king's ring, may not be reversed by any man."

9 Then the king's scribes were called at that time, in the third month, which is the month Sivan, on the twenty-third day of the month; and it was written according to all that Mordecai commanded to the Jews, and to the local governors, and the governors and princes of the provinces which are from India to Ethiopia, one hundred twenty-seven provinces, to every province according to its writing, and to every people in their language, and to the Jews in their writing, and in their language.

10 He wrote in the name of King Ahasuerus, and sealed it with the king's ring, and sent letters by courier on horseback, riding on royal horses that were bred from swift steeds.

11 In those letters, the king granted the Jews who were in every city to gather themselves together, and to defend their life, to destroy, to kill, and to cause to perish, all the power of the people and province that would assault them, their little ones and women, and to plunder their possessions,

12 on one day in all the provinces of King Ahasuerus, on the thirteenth day of the twelfth month, which is the month Adar.

13 A copy of the letter, that the decree should be given out in every province, was published to all the peoples, that the Jews should be ready for that day to avenge themselves on their enemies.

14 So the couriers who rode on royal horses went out, hastened and pressed on by the king's commandment. The decree was given out in the citadel of Susa.

15 Mordecai went out of the presence of the king in royal clothing of blue and white, and with a great crown of gold, and with a robe of fine linen and purple; and the city of Susa shouted and was glad.

16 The Jews had light, gladness, joy, and honor.

17 In every province, and in every city, wherever the king's commandment and his decree came, the Jews had gladness, joy, a feast, and a good day. Many from among the peoples of the land became Jews; for the fear of the Jews had fallen on them.

Chapter 8 Thoughts to Reflect Upon:

Have you ever seen God deliver justice on a broad scale? Have you ever found yourself doubtful of what God can do? Are you living under the old law or the new one God has written for you? Would you have done the same as Esther? How was God protecting you in your own time of persecution or trial? How did you feel after the persecution ended? How did you feel after reading this chapter? Did any verse stand out to you specifically?

Verse of the Day: 08/   Date:

_____

_____

_____

Journal/Notes Section-

_____

_____

_____

_____

_____

_____

_____

_____

CHAPTER 9
A GIANT REVERSAL

A nd so, Mordecai went from being a lowly person to a person of great fame, all because of the giant reversal of God. In God's kingdom, it pays to be loyal and righteous no matter how insignificant you are. "God chose the foolish things of the world that he might put to shame those who are wise. God chose the weak things of the world that he might put to shame the things that are strong" (1 Corinthians 1:27).

The tables are turned. The people of God are victorious. Those who wish to harm God's chosen people are instead being injured. Be encouraged that when an evil person tries to hurt you, when you refrain from avenging yourself but trust God, He will bring about justice: "For we know him who said, "Vengeance belongs to me. I will repay," says the Lord. Again, "The Lord will judge his people" (Hebrews 10:30).

In this chapter, we will see God destroy all the enemies of the Jewish people in all the provinces—hundreds of them. Now the king and all his resources are on their side. With this, they are unstoppable. Haman's ten sons will suffer the same fate as their father as they go to the gallows. Some might say Esther was too harsh by not showing love for her enemies, but sometimes there is no relenting. Esther displayed the same total victory we repeatedly see in the Old Testament.

You might say that the spirit of the Amalekites was in the DNA of Haman and his family. Interestingly, King Saul had been ordered to wipe them out entirely, but he disobeyed and spared King Agag:

"But Saul and the people spared Agag and the best of the sheep, of the cattle, of the fat calves, of the lambs, and all that was good, and were not willing to utterly destroy them; but everything that was vile and refuse, that they destroyed utterly" (1 Samuel 15:9).

Now you see how Haman evolved.

The final thought for this chapter has to do with Purim. It was decreed that the 14th and 15th days of the month of Adar were to be set apart as feast days to commemorate the Jews' victory over their enemies. The name is derived from *"pur"* (meaning "lot"), for when Haman determined to destroy the Jews, lots were cast to decide on which days to implement this.

Purim is celebrated among the Jews all over the world to this day. It's a festival remembered with charity for the less fortunate—a kind of Christmas without the commercials. We, too, celebrate with our Jewish family in remembering the faithfulness of God towards His people in times of trouble. When the flood of evil threatens our lives and values, we too will cry out to Him to raise a standard: "When the enemy shall come in like a flood, the Spirit of the Lord shall lift up a standard against him" (Isaiah 59:19 KJV).

Esther Chapter 9 Scripture

The Jews Have Victory

1 Now in the twelfth month, which is the month Adar, on the thirteenth day of the month, when the king's commandment and his decree came near to be put in execution, on the day that the enemies of

the Jews hoped to conquer them, (but it was turned out the opposite happened, that the Jews conquered those who hated them),

2 the Jews gathered themselves together in their cities throughout all the provinces of the King Ahasuerus, to lay hands on those who wanted to harm them. No one could withstand them, because the fear of them had fallen on all the people.

3 All the princes of the provinces, the local governors, the governors, and those who did the king's business helped the Jews, because the fear of Mordecai had fallen on them.

4 For Mordecai was great in the king's house, and his fame went out throughout all the provinces; for the man Mordecai grew greater and greater.

5 The Jews struck all their enemies with the stroke of the sword, and with slaughter and destruction, and did what they wanted to those who hated them.

6 In the citadel of Susa, the Jews killed and destroyed five hundred men.

7 They killed Parshandatha, Dalphon, Aspatha,

8 Poratha, Adalia, Aridatha, 9 Parmashta, Arisai, Aridai, and Vaizatha,

10 the ten sons of Haman the son of Hammedatha, the Jews' enemy, but they didn't lay their hand on the plunder.

11 On that day, the number of those who were slain in the citadel of Susa was brought before the king.

12 The king said to Esther the queen, "The Jews have slain and destroyed five hundred men in the citadel of Susa, including the ten sons of Haman; what then have they done in the rest of the king's provinces! Now what is your petition? It shall be granted you. What is your further request? It shall be done."

13 Then Esther said, "If it pleases the king, let it be granted to the Jews who are in Susa to do tomorrow also according to today's decree, and let Haman's ten sons be hanged on the gallows."

14 The king commanded this to be done. A decree was given out in Susa; and they hanged Haman's ten sons.

15 The Jews who were in Susa gathered themselves together on the fourteenth day also of the month Adar, and killed three hundred men in Susa; but they didn't lay their hand on the plunder.

16 The other Jews who were in the king's provinces gathered themselves together, defended their lives, had rest from their enemies, and killed seventy-five thousand of those who hated them; but they didn't lay their hand on the plunder.

17 This was done on the thirteenth day of the month Adar; and on the fourteenth day of that month they rested and made it a day of feasting and gladness.

18 But the Jews who were in Susa assembled together on the thirteenth and on the fourteenth days of the month; and on the fifteenth day of that month, they rested, and made it a day of feasting and gladness.

19 Therefore the Jews of the villages, who live in the unwalled towns, make the fourteenth day of the month Adar a day of gladness and feasting, a good day, and a day of sending presents of food to one another.

The Festival of Purim

20 Mordecai wrote these things, and sent letters to all the Jews who were in all the provinces of the king Ahasuerus, both near and far,

21 to enjoin them that they should keep the fourteenth and fifteenth days of the month Adar yearly,

22 as the days in which the Jews had rest from their enemies, and the month which was turned to them from sorrow to gladness, and from mourning into a good day; that they should make them days of feasting and gladness, and of sending presents of food to one another, and gifts to the needy.

23 The Jews accepted the custom that they had begun, as Mordecai had written to them;

24 because Haman the son of Hammedatha, the Agagite, the enemy of all the Jews, had plotted against the Jews to destroy them, and had cast "Pur", that is the lot, to consume them, and to destroy them;

25 but when this became known to the king, he commanded by letters that his wicked plan, which he had planned against the Jews, should return on his own head, and that he and his sons should be hanged on the gallows.

26 Therefore they called these days "Purim", from the word "Pur." Therefore because of all the words of this letter, and of that which they had seen concerning this matter, and that which had come to them,

27 the Jews established and imposed on themselves, and on their descendants, and on all those who joined themselves to them, so that it should not fail that they would keep these two days according to what was written, and according to its appointed time, every year;

28 and that these days should be remembered and kept throughout every generation, every family, every province, and every city; and that these days of Purim should not fail from among the Jews, nor their memory perish from their offspring.

29 Then Esther the queen, the daughter of Abihail, and Mordecai the Jew, wrote with all authority to confirm this second letter of Purim.

30 He sent letters to all the Jews, to the hundred twenty-seven provinces of the kingdom of Ahasuerus, with words of peace and truth,

31 to confirm these days of Purim in their appointed times, as Mordecai the Jew and Esther the queen had decreed, and as they had imposed upon themselves and their descendants, in the matter of the fastings and their cry.

32 The commandment of Esther confirmed these matters of Purim; and it was written in the book.

Chapter 9 Thoughts to Reflect Upon:

God often allows the bowls of wickedness to fill up before He delivers justice. Have you seen this happen before? Would you have shown more love to your enemies than Esther did? Do you believe God will avenge the people held captive today? Do you think God protects you? How did you feel after reading about this act of justice? How did you feel after reading this chapter? Did any verse stand out to you specifically?

Verse of the Day: 09/   Date:

_____

_____

_____

Journal/Notes Section-

_____

_____

_____

_____

_____

_____

_____

_____

_____

CHAPTER 10
OUR GOD REIGNS!

W e've reached the end, only to reverse the beginning. Esther is now queen, in place of Vashti, and God's people have been delivered and preserved. Mordecai is now a man of renown, and his name will be remembered forever in history. The plans of the evil one have come to naught, and God's people are vindicated.

Even in the darkest of times, we must remember that there is still reason to hope. No matter what happens in our world, we can trust that God's plans will come to pass. He will not leave us abandoned to the evils of the world. Jesus will return, and evil will be conquered once and for all. We will experience the perfect love, joy, and peace that exist in God's everlasting kingdom. We will have eternal life!

Let the story of Esther be a profound reminder to look past the momentary troubles of this age and toward the eternal life you have been promised in Jesus.

Esther Chapter 10 Scripture

Mordecai is Advanced to Greatness

1 King Ahasuerus laid a tribute on the land, and on the islands of the sea.

2 Aren't all the acts of his power and of his might, and the full account of the greatness of Mordecai, to which the king advanced him, written in the book of the chronicles of the kings of Media and Persia?

3 For Mordecai the Jew was next to King Ahasuerus, and great among the Jews, and accepted by the multitude of his brothers, seeking the good of his people, and speaking peace to all his descendants.

Chapter 10 Thoughts to Reflect Upon:

Do you think the tribute laid by King Ahasuerus was the hand of man or the hand of God? Have you ever been led to pay God tribute? What are the acts of God's power and might in your life? Do you believe people will tell your story? Are you aware of the impact you make on those around you? How did you feel after reading this book?

Verse of the Day: 10/   Date:

_____

_____

_____

Journal/Notes Section-

_____

_____

_____

_____

_____

_____

_____

CONCLUSION

The story of Esther vividly demonstrates God's hand in the life of a young girl and the Jewish people as He serves justice on the wicked. Esther and Mordecai were key partners in preserving God's people. They were both placed in this location and in this position for "such a time as this."

If you learn and remember one thing from this study, let it be this: God has placed you in your present time and location for "such a time as this." He has a divine purpose for your life that nothing can take away. All you have to do is trust Him and walk in that purpose. He will give you everything you need along the way to accomplish the task at hand.

In the midst of our trials, tribulations, and financial burdens, God is directing our every step. We must keep the virtue of obedience in our character to enable us to fulfill God's purpose. Being a Christian doesn't mean receiving a free pass from the trials of this life. Rather, it gives us a new perspective in which to see and process what we are experiencing. Esther and Mordecai didn't have it easy, even though they trusted God. Still, their faithfulness and obedience led them to victory in Christ. Let us follow in the footsteps of two of God's amazing people.

WANT MORE?

Building a relationship with my readers is the absolute best thing about writing. I occasionally send newsletters detailing new releases, special offers, and other news related to my *Guiding Scripture* series.

And if you sign up for the mailing list, I'll send you all this free material:

1   "A Guide to The Three Letters of John & Jude" – free eBook

2   "Daily Proverbs Checklist" –a checklist for the book of Proverbs

3   "5 Questions to Fully Understand a Bible Verse" – understanding what you are reading is vital; these questions will help.

4   "Leaders Daily Checklist" – God calls us to be leaders. We need to improve our leadership to set an example.

You can get the free eBook, Proverbs checklist, questions, and leadership checklist, by signing up at https://christophercoopersmith.com/guiding-scripture-series/

Did you learn something new?
Help other like-minded readers find this book.

Reviews are the most powerful tools in my arsenal for getting my books connected to other like-minded readers. I do not have the same financial resources as a larger publishing house.

However, I do have something much more valuable: **a dedicated group of readers who support my work.**

Honest reviews from my readers help my books gain the attention of new audiences.

If you've enjoyed this book, would you kindly consider leaving a review on the relevant page? Even a short review can make a big difference in helping me reach more readers.

Thank you for your support!

Click here to leave a short one-minute review.

Or Scan This QR

AUTHOR

I'm a sinner redeemed by Christ's grace. God has fueled a passionate fire in me to build a Christ-centered community. I have had the privilege of serving the community both locally and abroad. To date, I have spread the good news in over 11 different countries. My one true purpose is to use my God-given gifts to lead others to redemption.

You can send an email to gs@christophercoopersmith.com to join our private Facebook group to establish a Christian community around God's wisdom. I hope you enjoy this journal.

For those of you who are brave enough, tell me what you think about this book.

Email: gs@christophercoopersmith.com.

I am for real. I am an actual human being and read every email I get. So don't be surprised if you receive an email response from me!

OTHER TITLES BY CHRISTOPHER COOPERSMITH

Have you read them all?

The Three Letters of John & Jude

This Journey through the Letters of John and Jude provides a roadmap to developing a deeper understanding of scripture and all God's teachings. Like a salve for the soul, it is filled with much-needed wisdom, lessons, and stories that will resonate with you and what's happening in your life.

Read this book for free scanning this QR

Proverbs: The Blessings of Wisdom

The Blessings of Wisdom is a chapter-by-chapter discussion of those enlightened and fulfilling Old Testament maxims. Using uplifting personal stories and pre-prepared writing pages to encourage reflection, Coopersmith helps turn the printed text into vivid, actionable knowledge. And after adding his detailed analysis to your Bible study routine, you'll be able to see God's power and blessings move in your everyday life.

Read now scanning this QR

Hebrews: Christ Never Leaves Us

Christ Never Leaves Us is a meticulous examination of the themes, reassurances, and admonitions contained in this missive to new Messianic converts. Using journal questions and comprehensive scripture references, Coopersmith reveals how to lean on messages to ancient Christians for hope in your modern-day walk with Jehovah. And by pouring through this study with an open heart, you'll soon be hearing God's voice with crystal clarity.

Read now scanning this QR

ACKNOWLEDGMENTS

This book is dedicated to my bonus family for always being great friends to me. Our beautiful family consists of Andrew, his daughter Anastasia, Robyn, and their mother Cathrine, not forgetting their two dogs, Spike and Hope. Thank you for being a part of my life. When I was in need, you were there for me. It is a blessing to receive your support throughout the years. We will always have wonderful times and memories to share. You are a strong, Christ-centered family and I am thankful to be part of it. It is truly remarkable how you give without any thought of receiving. It is my belief our Lord is blessing you for your good deeds. Your love for me strengthens my faith, and I am a better Christian today because of your love. May God be with you always!

Copyright 2023

Editor: Zachary Wessell
Copy Editor: Fleur Vaz & Vickie Spencer
Proofreader: Kerrie McLoughlin & Changfang Wang
Cover Design: Damonza.com
eBook: ISBN – 978-1-955922-18-0
Paperback: ISBN – 978-1-955922-19-7
Hardcover: ISBN – 978-1-955922-20-3

BIBLIOGRAPHY

Agape Bible Study. "The Book of Ruth - Lesson 1: Introduction and Chapter 1 Ruth Entrusts Her Life to Naomi," 2012. https://www.agapebiblestudy.com/Ruth/Ruth_Lesson_1.htm.

———. "The Book of Ruth - Lesson 2: Chapters 2:1-3:5 Ruth's Life in Bethlehem," 2012. https://www.agapebiblestudy.com/Ruth/Ruth_Lesson_2.htm.

Bible Study Ministry. "Ruth Chapter 2 Summary: Chapter Summaries." Accessed April 16, 2022. https://biblestudyministry.com/ruth-chapter-2-summary-chapter-summaries/.

———. "Ruth Chapter 3 Summary: Chapter Summaries." Accessed April 16, 2022. https://biblestudyministry.com/ruth-chapter-3-summary-chapter-summaries/.

Enduring Word. "Esther 1 – a Queen Is Deposed," 2018. https://enduringword.com/bible-commentary/esther-1/.

———. "Esther 3 – Haman's Conspiracy," 2018. https://enduringword.com/bible-commentary/esther-3/.

———. "Ruth 2 – Ruth's Work as a Gleaner," 2018. https://enduringword.com/bible-commentary/ruth-2/.

ESV.org. "The Global Message of Esther." Accessed April 16, 2022. https://www.esv.org/resources/esv-global-study-bible/global-message-of-esther/.

Nielson, Kathleen. "Knowing the Bible: Ruth and Esther." The
  Gospel Coalition, 2015.
  https://www.thegospelcoalition.org/course/knowing-the-bible-
  ruth-and-esther/#week-12-summary-and-conclusion.

Snyder, Airelle. "Ruth Chapter 3," February 26, 2018.
  http://www.airellesnyder.com/ruth-chapter-3/#/.

TOW Project. "Conclusions About the Book of Ruth." Theology of
  Work. Accessed April 16, 2022.
  https://www.theologyofwork.org/old-testament/ruth-and-
  work/conclusions-about-the-book-of-ruth.

Zavada, Jack. "Meet Ruth: Great Grandmother of King David." *Learn
  Religions*, September 5, 2019.
  https://www.learnreligions.com/ruth-ancestor-of-jesus-701194.

Hayford, Jack W. NKJV, Spirit-Filled Life Bible. 3rd ed. Thomas
Nelson Publishers, 2018.

Made in the USA
Coppell, TX
03 July 2024

34237265R00069